M000006886

Foolish Questions

GREETINGS & SALUTATIONS !

FOOLISH QUESTIONS

WITH DUE THANKS
TO THE NEW YORK
EVENING MAIL

BY R. GOLDBERG

Coachwhip Publications
Landisville, Pennsylvania

Foolish Questions, by Rube Goldberg
2009 Coachwhip Publications
Original publication date: 1909

ISBN 1-930585-84-5
ISBN-13 978-1-930585-84-3

CoachwhipBooks.com

All Rights Reserved. No part of this publication may be reproduced, stored in a retrieval system or transmitted in any form or by any means—electronic, mechanical, photocopy, recording or any other—except for brief quotations in printed reviews, without the prior permission of the author or publisher.

FOOLISH FOREWORD

A YOUNG MAN AND A YOUNG LADY ARE SEATED IN THE PARLOR - THE YOUNG MAN ON THE YOUNG LADY'S SOFA AND THE YOUNG LADY ON THE YOUNG MAN'S LAP. AS IS THE CUSTOM IN HUMAN SOCIETY, THEY ARE ENGAGED IN A LITTLE GAME OF THAT HARMLESS AND INEXPENSIVE INDOOR SPORT KNOWN AS OSCULATION.

THE YOUNG LADY'S MOTHER, GREATLY CONCERNED OVER THE SAFETY OF HER CONSTANCE, APPEARS IN THE DOORWAY AND ASKS WITH NATURAL INDIGNATION, "YOUNG MAN, ARE YOU KISSING MY DAUGHTER?"

THE YOUNG - BUT WHAT'S THE USE OF STRINGING THIS OUT? YOU'LL RUN ACROSS HIS ANSWER TO MAMMA'S QUERY IN A MINUTE.

THE PUBLISHERS, WISHING TO PLACE THE CUSTOMARY BUNCH OF WORDS AT THE BEGINNING OF THIS - WHATEVER YOU MAY CHOOSE TO CALL IT - ASKED ME TO SPILL A LITTLE CHATTER ABOUT THE ORIGIN OF THE IDEA UPON WHICH THE PICTURES ARE BASED. HENCE THE OPENING RAVE. IT HAS NOTHING TO DO WITH MY FIRST HAZY IDEAS UPON THE SUBJECT, BUT VERY ABLY FULFILLS THE MISSION OF TAKING UP SPACE ON THIS PAGE.

WHILE EATING IS STILL IN VOGUE, I SALAAM BEFORE THE MENU - THE PUBLISHERS ARE MY COLLECTIVE MEAL TICKET.

I WISH TO CALL THE READER'S SPECIAL ATTENTION TO THE NUMERALS UNDER THE PICTURES. THEY ARE VERY IMPORTANT BECAUSE THEY MEAN NOTHING.

I HEREBY ACKNOWLEDGE MY DEEP APPRECIATION OF THE GREAT HELP THE FOLLOWING WORKS HAVE BEEN TO ME IN CONCOCTING THIS MODEST JOY TONIC :- JOSIAH S. TALCUM'S "PREHISTORIC GOULASH"; OLAF GOOK'S "THE CAREER OF A PILL"; J. HECTOR BEZITZ'S "ONIONS I HAVE MET"; LUCIAN CAVIAR'S "MONOTONY"; AND Q. ERASMUS BOOB'S "EVOLUTION OF INDIGESTION".

PLEASE PASS OUT ON THE RIGHT AND DON'T FORGET TO SEE THE TWO-HEADED ZEBRA IN THE NEXT TENT.

R.G.

CELL 41144

5

To my friend,
"Franklin P. Adams,
who made this book
possible.

IS THIS A BLOT?

FOOLISH QUESTIONS - NO. 7

FOOLISH QUESTIONS- NO.16.

FOOLISH QUESTIONS- NO.17.

FOOLISH QUESTIONS— NO. 21.

FOOLISH QUESTIONS - NO. 28.

FOOLISH QUESTIONS - NO. 30.

FOOLISH QUESTIONS - NO. 34.

FOOLISH QUESTIONS - NO. 36.

31

FOOLISH QUESTIONS - NO. 1,372.

35

FOOLISH QUESTIONS — NO. 1,374.

FOOLISH QUESTIONS — NO. 1,382.

FOOLISH QUESTIONS—NO. 1,383.

FOOLISH QUESTIONS—NO. 1,391

FOOLISH QUESTIONS — NO. 1,404.

FOOLISH QUESTIONS—No. 1413.

FOOLISH QUESTIONS—NO. 1414.

FOOLISH QUESTIONS — NO. 1419.

FOOLISH QUESTIONS—NO. 1421.

FOOLISH QUESTIONS—NO. 1427.

FOOLISH QUESTIONS—NO. 3,001.

FOOLISH QUESTIONS - NO. 153,698.

FOOLISH QUESTIONS – NO. 153,702.

·FINIS·